How to b
BIG

Using Controversial Common Sense

First published in 2006 by Timpson Limited. © John Timpson 2006.

ISBN 0-9547049-7-5

Timpson House Claverton Road Wythenshawe Manchester M23 9TT
Tel: 0161 946 6200 www.timpson.com
Written by John Timpson CBE. Illustrated by Robert Barrow. Printed in Great Britain.

Managing the business upside-down

We run our business in a strange way, we call it 'upside-down management'.

Delegate

Trust your employees to get on and do
their job, but still take responsibility.

No Rules

Don't issue orders – give advice. Running a business is not a dictatorship, so don't tell your managers how to do their job.

Encourage Initiative

Give your people the freedom to try ideas.
If the latest initiative doesn't work, don't
criticise, the next idea might be a winner.

Banish Bureaucracy

Government creates enough paperwork without us producing more red tape inside the business. Administrators seldom increase sales but they always add to the costs.

Act like a small business

Avoid the trappings of the big companies. You don't need a department of corporate planning and communication – do it yourself.

Don't be paralysed by analysis

Most long reports are boring – just read the summary – it will tell you all you need to know.

Beware of budgets

Let your finance team draw up the budget while you get on and improve the business. If you let everyone loose on budgets they will abandon their normal job and play politics. Your role is to check the final draft and make sure that the budget they've produced is sensible.

Hate Meetings

Some meetings are useful, but most waste a lot of time and money. Do you really know how much time your people spend in meetings?

Resist Consultants

Only use consultants for a job that no one in the business can do. Make sure they leave as soon as the job is done.

Beware of market research

All the findings on the opposite page would have got us into trouble. Find things out by walking the business, talking to colleagues and meeting customers face to face.

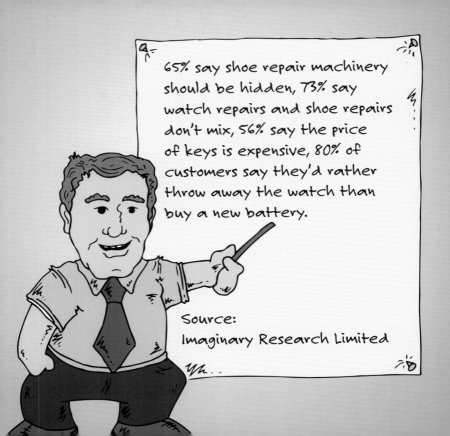

Police the politics

Watch the people who promote their own importance, they could be pushing their selfish aims at the expense of the business. Show you can't be manipulated.

Pick great people

The future of the business is in the hands of its people, pick personalities that will create a great company. Great businesses have great people – the drongos work elsewhere.

Pick Personalities

A CV only comes to life when you meet
someone face-to-face. Take note of the
candidates experience and their references,
but base your final decision on their personality.

Take a chance

Don't always pick the safe option – give yourself the benefit of a diverse team – it will make the business more exiting.

Promote from within

Create a management training scheme
that gives you the chance of filling every
job from within the company.

Keep looking for ideas

A business makes progress by doing different things, your job is to collect new ideas and pick the ones which will work.

Aim to be the best

You must aim for excellence – no matter how good you are you can always get better. So your job is never done.

Love Change

If you like the easy life you won't become a big boss. Success comes from daring to be different and your job is to promote the change agenda.

Talk to the people close to the action

Meet the people who are nearest to your product – salesmen, operatives and customers. They know more about your business than the Finance Director.

Walk the office

When you are in the office don't spend all day sat behind your desk. Go walk-about with a smile on your face and chat to the people who have a more boring job – but can teach you a lot about the business.

Know every shop

Aim to visit every shop, every year. The more you know the shops, the more you know the business and the more chance you have of finding ideas.

Meet the bright sparks

Make a special point of talking to the people
who have something worthwhile to say – 2% of
your people will produce 99% of the ideas.

Earn *success* time and again

Success is short lived – to gain a great reputation, you need to win again and again.

Don't accept mediocrity

"It'll do", won't do. Once you accept a substandard performance you have limited the ability of your company to grow.

Do the big thinking

You must create the big plan so everyone knows
where the company is going. Create enough time
to identify the problems and pick the solutions.
You can't delegate the strategy.

Avoid day-to-day management

Delegate all the day-to-day tasks so you are always free to give the future of the business all the attention it needs.

Have a guru

Make sure you have at least one person
who can give you unbiased advice.
Timpson gurus include our non-executive
directors and the Chairman's wife.

Identify your strengths

Businesses make money by being better than their competitors – decide what your company is good at and how you can take advantage of your strengths.

Define Success

Ambition should be much more than beating budget. List all the things you would like to achieve like having the best looking shops on the high street and being a great place to work.

TIMPSON
The Quality Service People
Customer Service
Champion

Stick to the main business

You will often be tempted to spend your time on new ventures – but never neglect the core business – that is where you make the money.

Pick the priorities

Most people give every decision the same level of importance – it's your job to sort out the priorities.

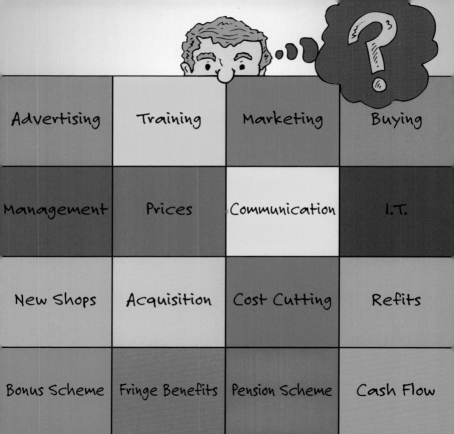

Use common sense

Running a business is a lot less complicated
than most people would like to imagine –
most successful companies display a large
amount of common sense.

Computer Modeling

In-Depth Research

Corporate Planning Dept Review

The Art Of Plain Thinking

Make it simple

The shorter your strategy the more powerful it will become – so keep it brief and keep it simple.

Put it in pictures

Your thinking will only become worthwhile when your strategy is communicated. Write it in a way others can easily understand by using pictures as well as words.

Do it again

The thinking job never ends. Keep worrying about the business and be prepared to change your plans.

Paranoid about profit

You are in business to make money, so profit is the real measure of your success – keep searching for ways to improve your bottom line.

Check cash every day

The bank balance gives you a daily measure of your performance – always compare the cash with the same day last year – and explain the difference.

Cost conscious culture

Set the style by demonstrating a prudent approach to spending money.

Unnecessary extravagance has no place in any part of the business.

Don't Overpay

Never be so blinded by ambition that you pay over the odds. If the price is too high walk away and wait for the next opportunity.

Look under every stone

Be a detective and search for the little clues that might lead to big savings. If you spot something unusual it could be hiding a mammoth waste of money.

Identify useless expenditure

The perfect way to prune costs is to cut out things the business doesn't need. Every company incurs some useless expenditure – can you spot the activities that can be eliminated and never be missed?

Delegate cost control

Your people are much better than you at controlling costs. Give them the job through a bonus based on profit – so they get a percentage of the money they save.

It's your decision

Our system of upside-down management doesn't delegate the responsibility to make the big decisions – that's your job.

Control Cap-Ex

Don't let anyone else invest your money
– the choice of capital projects will
determine the future of the business.

Negotiate the deals

Acquisitions and disposals will play a vital part in your future fortunes – make sure you are at the negotiating table.

Make up your mind slowly

You will seldom need to make an instant decision. If you have time to make up your mind, take it – until the answer is clear.

Take easy decisions

To save a lot of time and bother take the obvious decisions and leave the difficult problems until you know the answer.

Clear away obstacles

Use the power of your position to clear
any obstacles that prevent your team
doing their job.

Do it now

If you know the answer why wait – put your plans into action straight away – it saves time and stops you worrying.

I'll do it next week
Let me think on it
It's on my list
Let him sweat on it
I don't want to rush
I'll talk to George first

Stick to a good decision

You are surrounded by sceptics ready to give advice and put doubt in your mind. Have the courage of your conviction and show you have the character of a true entrepreneur.

Never make a decision at a meeting

Meetings can be useful to communicate facts and exchange views, but they are never the place to take irreversible decisions.

Have the courage to overrule management

You give your people lots of authority but you don't have to agree with everyone – our business is not a democracy. Don't allow peer pressure to stop you taking a decision you know is right. Other people may have a different agenda.

Overrule the rule makers

Don't let petty regulations run your business – if you follow every bureaucrat's bulletin to the letter you will have no time or money left to run your business. Challenge any silly legislation and make your own rules.

If in doubt – do nothing

You always have 3 choices – yes, no and maybe. If you can't make up your mind delay your decision until you can. It's often better to sleep on it.

Take calculated risks

You can't play safe all the time, entrepreneurs have to take some risks to stay ahead of their competitors – but don't be foolish – only take risks when the odds are heavily stacked in your favour.

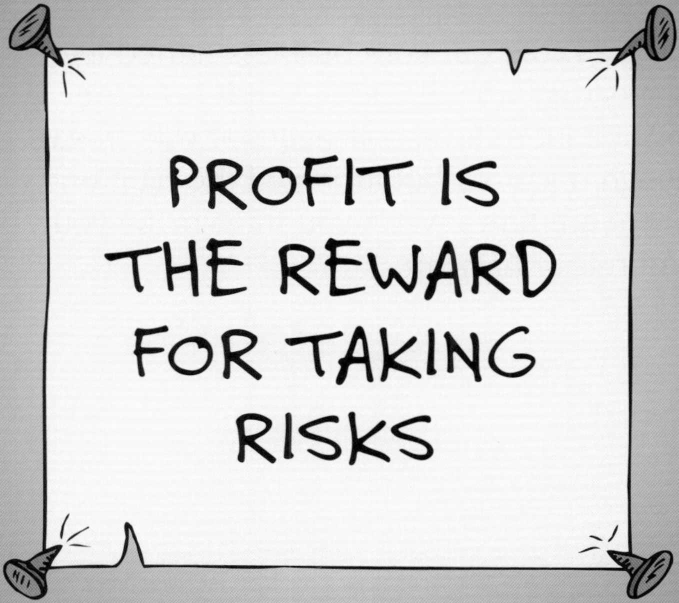
PROFIT IS THE REWARD FOR TAKING RISKS

Don't be sentimental

In 1987 I sold our core business started by my great-grandfather, and with it I put the jobs of a lot of loyal colleagues at risk. It was a tough decision, but it proved the right one – there are times when you must make your head rule your heart.

Make Mistakes

No one is perfect – you are bound to get it wrong some of the time, but never sweep your mistakes under the carpet – hold your hands up and put it down as experience.

Don't waste time on things you can't influence

Before putting your brain to work make sure it is worth the effort. Only tackle problems where you can make a difference.

Communicator in chief

Your ideas will only work if your people know about them and agree with you. To make ideas come true you must get the message across.

Set the style

You have more influence than you realise –
the whole organisation will listen to your
words and follow your example.

Be Yourself

Don't cover up your personality by putting on an act – reveal your true self and be totally natural. People trust bosses with a human touch.

Turn your strategy into a crusade

Bring your important ideas to life by giving them lots of character. It's important that everyone knows where the company is going, so make the strategy memorable and make it fun.

Create your own media

When you become a chief executive you also take on the roles of journalist and film producer. Memos and emails don't give your message the magic touch. You need to use imagination to grab everyone's attention.

Win hearts and minds

Your job is to get everyone to believe in your ideas – the plan is much more likely to succeed if it is backed by their enthusiasm.

Entertain

Be prepared to develop your social skills because the job involves plenty of parties with you as the host – help your people celebrate success.

Be involved in training

More messages are passed round the business during training courses than by any managers meeting or memo. Make sure the training team are getting your message across.

Be your consumers' champion

Consumer care and consumer satisfaction will have a big influence on your success – fight the battle on your customers' behalf and help improve the business.

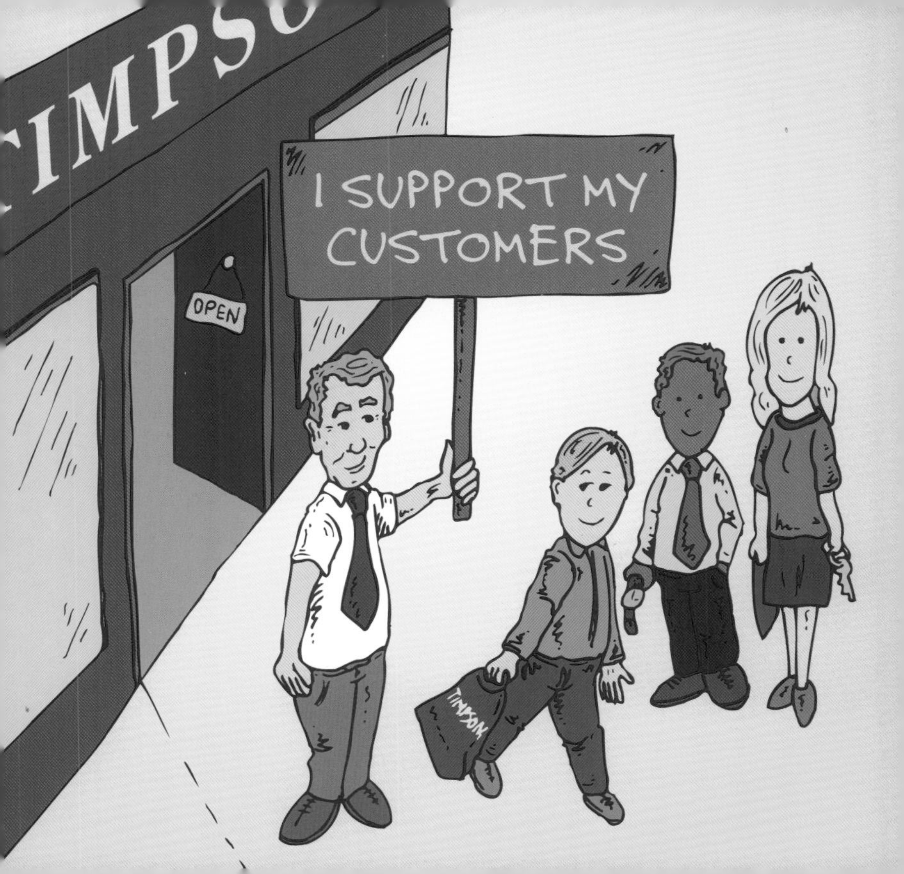
TIMPSO
I SUPPORT MY CUSTOMERS
OPEN
TIMPSON

Take time to sell ideas

Don't expect your people to pick up your ideas in a few minutes – it takes years to change the culture of a business, so be patient.

Repeat the message

If you have something important to say – say it again and again. The first time people hear the message, the next time they might understand it and after a few times they might believe in it.

SALESMANSHIP SALESMANSHIP
SALESMANSHIP SALESMANSHIP
SALESMANSHIP SALESMANSHIP
SALESMANSHIP SALESMANSHIP
SALESMANSHIP SALESMANSHIP
SALESMANSHIP SALESMANSHIP
SALESMANSHI ALESMANSHIP
SALESMANSH ALESMANSHIP
SALESMANSHIP SALESMANSHIP
SALESMANSHIP SALESMANSHIP
SALESMANSHIP SALESMANSHIP
SALESMANSHIP SALESMANSHIP

No Drongo's

Poor people do a lot of damage to a business – they undermine morale, annoy your superstars and cost a lot of money in the process. Although it's very irritating to pay compensation, paying a financial farewell to a drongo is always money well spent.

Don't waste time on difficult people

Managers can spend lots of their time with people who are useless – disciplinary hearings, retraining and counselling. Abandon the lost causes and spend your time with the people who can make you more money.

Avoid prima donnas

Pompous big headed loud mouths are as irritating to the rest of your team as they are to you. Don't be intimidated by the claim to be indispensable – say goodbye as soon as possible.

Over Promoted

Sadly, from time-to-time you will make a mistake and promote someone to a job too far. Step in straight away and move them to a role more suited to their talents. Remember it was your fault they were given the wrong job.

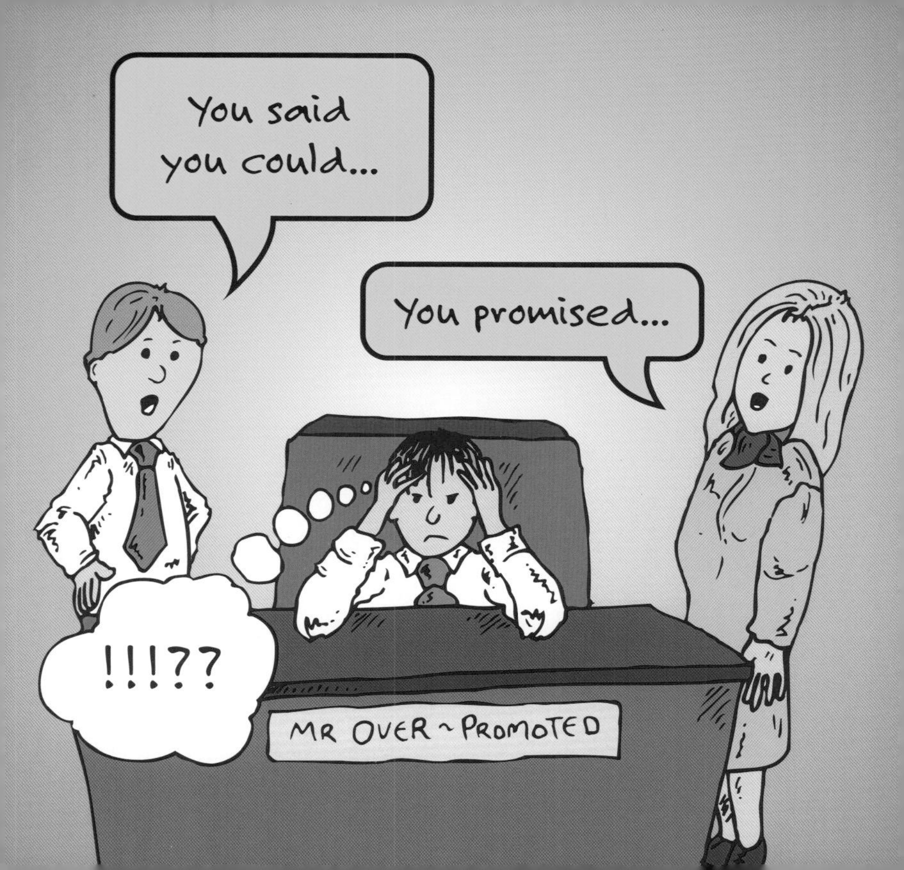
You said you could...
You promised...
!!!??
MR OVER ~ PROMOTED

No Fudging

If someone is promoted beyond their ability put them back to their old level or say a generous goodbye – don't set them another impossible task or send them down a blind alley.

You can't hide a joker by shuffling the pack

Don't try and hide poor people by giving them a dead end job – the rest of your organisation will resent the salary they are paid and you will waste time creating their new job. In the end it catches up with you.

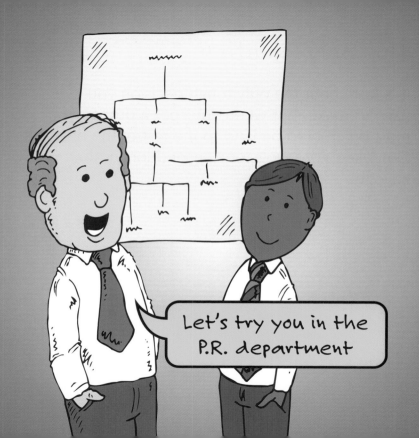

The only solution

It is just about the only tough decision you ever have to make, but when you spot a drongo you must be cruel to be kind to the rest of the business. Don't keep drongo's for a second longer than you have to.

Pamper your people

Give your good people all the riches you can afford – remember they are the people that make you the money – give them a decent share in their success.

Trust everyone and watch them carefully

Follow upside-down management, trust your people and give them the space to do amazing things – but keep a close check on what they are doing. You are responsible for spotting their good ideas and putting things right if there is a problem.

Be loyal to your people

You have a special relationship with the members of your team – in return for their trust – fight battles on their behalf.

Support the mavericks

People who break the rules often provide the best ideas. Look after your eccentrics they might show you how to grow the business.

Be an advice bureau

One of your most important jobs is to listen and find out how you can help your people do even better.

Encourage care for others

You know you are creating the right
atmosphere when your colleagues start
helping other members of the team.
Aim to develop a big family of friends.

Find loads of ways to reward success

Make your star performers feel really special by recognising their best moments with special praise. Have lots of ways to say well done – great achievements deserve to be recognised by a truly individual moment.

Personalise Praise

If you are marking an individual
achievement, do it in an individual way.
Show you care by going to the trouble of
producing your own personal tribute.

Well done letters

Emails have put a premium on hand written letters.
Pick up a proper pen, use real ink, write the
envelope to your winner's home address and stick
on the stamp – and if possible enclose a cheque.
That's praise indeed.

Pay for success

If your business does well you deserve some credit – but never forget the people who made it happen and show your appreciation with pound notes.

Pay the best better

Make sure your best people get the most money. Some people believe in equal pay, but a good business puts the high performers on a premium rate.

Share the spoils

Every year there are people in the business who make a big difference – sadly some never come to your attention. But if you do spot a superstar make a fuss of them and do it with money.

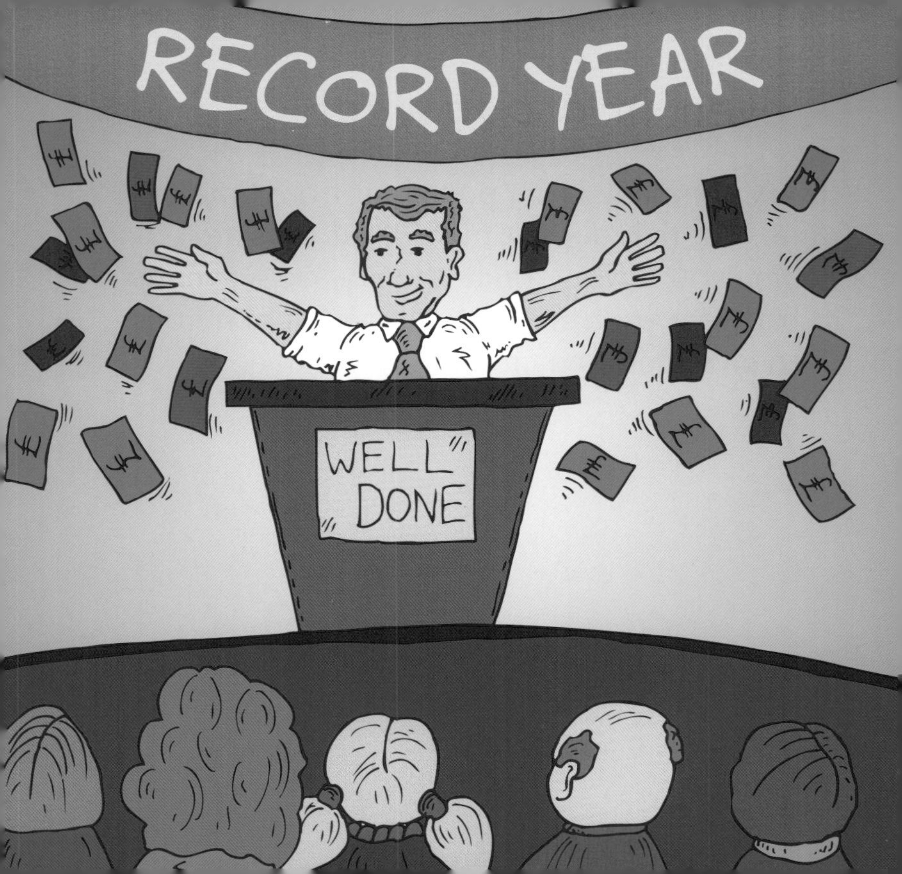
RECORD YEAR
WELL DONE

...even in a bad year

Every company has a poor year from time-to-time, but that doesn't mean your stars are letting you down – quite the reverse – even in a bad year your business will be full of heroes – so give them the credit they deserve.

No wage freeze

Wage freezes are a bad idea. Don't cut the real pay of your best people and tempt them to join the opposition – instead, eliminate the cost of paying drongos. Bad times give you the chance to cut out the poor performers.

Bonus Scheme

Make sure everyone has the benefit of a bonus scheme. It's the best way to link their working life to the success of the company.

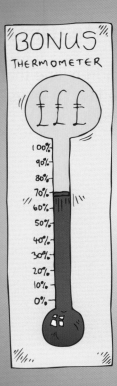

A business full of entrepreneurs

Our bonus scheme created an adrenaline that has run through the business for the last 10 years – increasing pay and increasing profit.

Final Thoughts

I have left three vital points to the end and three fundamental principles that should help you to keep your feet on the ground and stick to common sense.

Don't follow the crowd

Bureaucrats and accountants take pride in sticking to rules – entrepreneurs make money by breaking new ground. Don't be restricted by convention – ignore the majority and do it your way.

Compare with last year

Finance directors often only compare performance with budget – it puts them in control. Ruin their day and insist that every figure is compared with last year.

FINANCIAL REVIEW

SALES (£000S)	THIS YEAR	%	LAST YEAR	%
SHOE REPAIRS	31,857	32	28,874	30
KEY CUTTING	31,599	32	29,404	31
ENGRAVING	7,834	8	7,518	8
WATCH/JEWELLERY REPAIRS	9,126	9	8,537	9
DRY CLEANING	4,219	4	5,512	6
MERCHANDISE	12,510	13	15,864	17
TOTAL	97,145	98	95,709	100
HOUSE NAMEPLATE	2,161	2		
	99,306	100	95,709	100

COSTS

WAGES	35,327	36	36,180	38
PROPERTY	18,679	19	18,672	20
MATERIALS	7,656	8	10,473	11
OTHER COSTS	9,821	10	8,669	9
VAT	14,611	15	14,585	15
TOTAL	86,093	89	88,579	93
NET TRADING PROFIT	11,052	11	7,130	7

INVESTMENT

Last year profit adjusted for one off's etc. and includes Sainsbury trading for branches closed in this year.

REFITS	1,450	4,550
MACHINERY	750	1,050
NEW SHOPS/HQ/WHITE EAGLE	1,600	1,000
	3,800	6,600

Make a list

No one has a perfect memory and you remember less and less as you get older. Don't leave things to chance – make sure you don't miss a trick by keeping an action list.

Have Fun

If you don't enjoy the business – go and do something else. Having fun is a vital part of any successful business.

Be Lucky

Every successful business needs a lucky break –
we have had lots of them. Have the courage to
take advantage of your good fortune.

Never be surprised

Always expect the unexpected – life is unpredictable and it is people who provide the biggest surprises. Don't take anyone for granted.